Crafting with Nature

GET DIRTY!

Science and Craft Projects with Soil and Rocks

By Ruth Owen

Enslow PUBLISHING

Published in 2024 by Enslow Publishing, LLC
2544 Clinton Street
Buffalo, NY 14224

Portions of this work were originally authored by Ruth Owen and published as *Science and Craft Projects with Rocks and Soil*. All new material this edition authored by Ruth Owen.

Produced for Rosen by Ruby Tuesday Books Ltd
Editor for Ruby Tuesday Books Ltd: Mark J. Sachner
Designer: Emma Randall

Manufactured in the United States of America

CPSIA compliance information: Batch #CSENS24: For further information contact Enslow Publishing LLC, New York, New York at 1-800-398-2504.

Please visit our website, www.enslowpublishing.com. For a free color catalog of all our high-quality books, call toll free 1-800-398-2504 or fax 1-877-980-4454.

Cataloging-in-Publication Data

Names: Owen, Ruth.
Title: Get dirty!: science and craft projects with soil and rocks / Ruth Owen.
Description: New York : Enslow Publishing, 2024. | Series: Crafting with nature | Includes glossary and index.
Identifiers: ISBN 9781978535602 (pbk.) | ISBN 9781978535619 (library bound) | ISBN 9781978535626 (ebook)
Subjects: LCSH: Rocks--Juvenile literature. | Soils--Juvenile literature. | Rock craft--Juvenile literature.
Classification: LCC QE432.2 O94 2024 | DDC 552.0078--dc23

Photo Credits:
Cover, 1, 4–5, 6–7, 8, 9 (center), 10, 11 (top), 11 (bottom), 14–15, 16–17, 18–19, 21 (bottom), 22–23, 26–27 © Shutterstock; 9, 12–13, 20–21, 24–25, 28–29 © Ruby Tuesday Books Ltd; 11 (center) © Simm Sepp, Wikipedia Creative Commons.

CONTENTS

OUR PLANET ROCKS!

Our planet is completely covered with a thick layer, or crust, of rock. When we look at a mountain, the Grand Canyon, or a magnificent rock formation such as El Capitan, we are actually looking at a part of that rocky crust.

When we dig the soil in a garden or visit a beach, we usually find rock. But how do all these rocks form? Do they all have different names? And why are some rocks more precious than others?

The El Capitan rock formation in Yosemite National Park

This book has all the answers to these rocking questions and many more! It is packed with great facts and you will also have the chance to get hands-on with rocks by doing some cool, rocky crafts.

pebbles on a beach

This piece of rock has precious green emeralds in it.

Sorting Rocks

There are hundreds of different types of rocks. Scientists and rock collectors sort rocks into three main groups called **igneous rocks**, **sedimentary rocks**, and **metamorphic rocks**.

HOW DOES IGNEOUS ROCK FORM?

How do scientists and rock collectors know if a rock is an igneous, sedimentary, or metamorphic rock? One way is to look at how the rock formed.

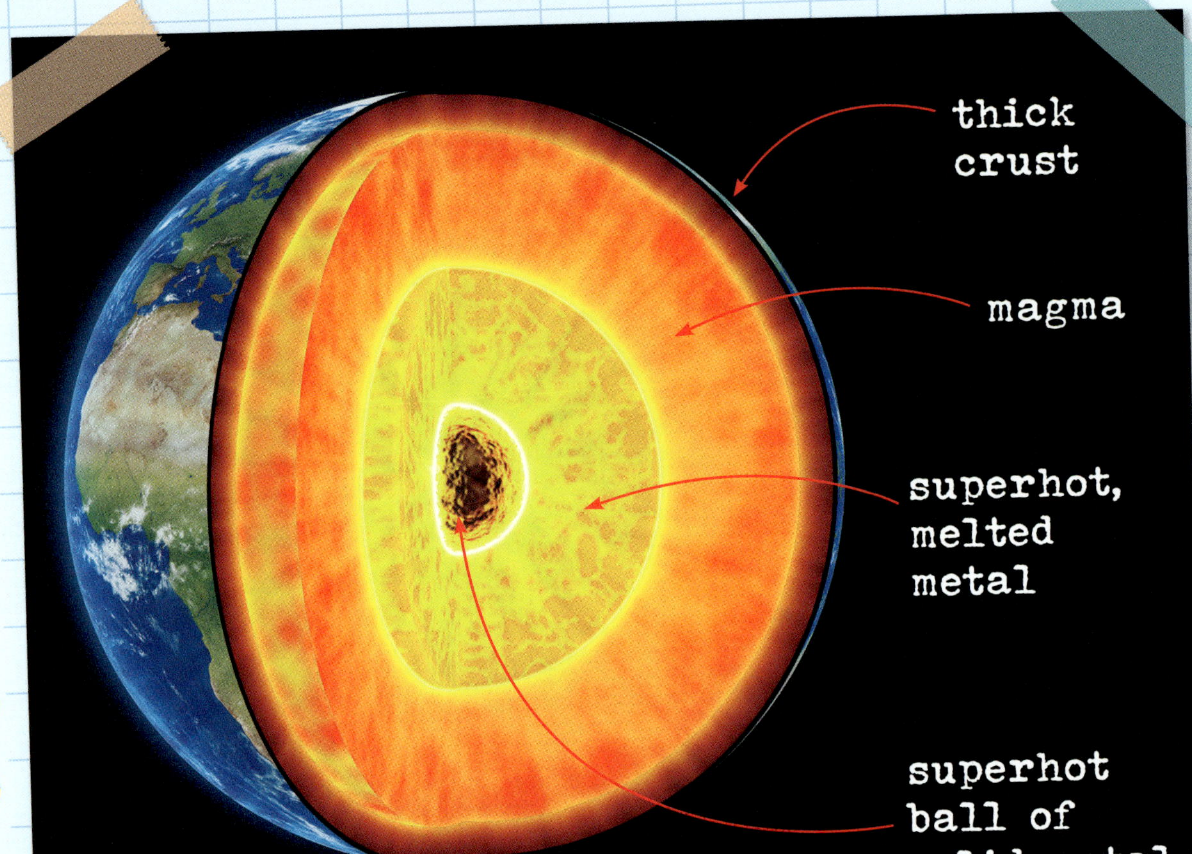

This picture shows what's inside Earth.

Igneous rock forms in two ways. The first way happens when a **volcano** erupts.

Below the Earth's crust is an area called the mantle. Here it is so hot that the rock becomes soft like toffee. This soft, melted rock is called **magma**.

Sometimes, during a volcanic eruption, magma from inside Earth explodes or pours out of a volcano. Once the hot magma is outside of the volcano, it is known as **lava**. As the lava cools, it gets hard and becomes igneous rock.

an erupting volcano

Igneous Rock under the Ground

Sometimes, magma oozes up into cracks in Earth's crust. Then the magma cools, turns hard, and becomes igneous rock that's under the ground.

This obsidian rock is made of lava from a volcano.

This granodiorite rock formed underground from magma.

ROCK ANIMAL SCULPTURES

Rock has been used as a material for making sculptures since ancient times. Sculptors cut and carve statues of people, animals, and shapes from chunks of natural rock. In this first craft project, you will make mini rock sculptures from pebbles.

You will need:

- Pebbles and rocks
- A small brush
- Warm water and soap
- Modeling clay
- Strong glue (check on packaging if suitable)
- Acrylic paint
- Paintbrushes
- Clear varnish (available online and from craft stores)
- An adult teammate to go pebble hunting with you

GET CRAFTING:

1. You can find pebbles at the beach or at the edges of a lake or river. Ask friends, neighbors, or family members if you can go pebble hunting in their gardens, too. You can also buy pebbles from garden centers.

2. Look at the shapes of the pebbles you find and be inspired by their shapes to get creative!

3. Use the small brush to scrub the pebbles clean in warm water and soap. Then allow them to dry.

4 If you are making a sculpture with more than one pebble, test out your idea first. Join the pebbles together with little blobs of modeling clay.

5 Glue the pebbles together. Follow the instructions on the glue's packaging. While the glue dries, you can help the pebbles stay in place by wedging modeling clay around them.

6 When the glue is dry, paint your model.

7 Sometimes, the natural colors of pebbles can work really well. The rock dog in the photograph here was made using white stones. The brown spots were then painted on.

HOW DOES SEDIMENTARY ROCK FORM?

The clue to how sedimentary rock forms is in its name—sediment. This kind of rock is made from tiny grains of rock called sediment. So where does sediment come from?

sediment may only be the size of a grain of sugar or a speck of dust.

Rock may be hard, but wind and rain can wear it away. As wind blows past a large rock or rainwater washes over it, tiny pieces break off.

On the seashore, waves crash against rock cliffs and break off tiny pieces. All these tiny pieces of rock become sediment.

Sand is a type of sediment. If you look at sand through a magnifying glass, you will see it is made from billions of tiny pieces of rock!

What Is Dirt Made of?

Dirt, or soil, in gardens is made from tiny pieces of rock. It looks different than sand because it contains other ingredients. Soil also has tiny pieces of dead plants and animals mixed up with the rock.

COLORED SAND PAPERWEIGHTS

Paperweights are fun decorations for a desk or shelf. They are also useful for keeping stacks of papers under control. These colorful paperweights are made from layers of sand in recycled containers.

You will need:

- Clear bottles or jars with lids
- Sand from a toy or craft store
- Waxed paper
- Cutting board
- Colored chalk
- Small bowls (one for each color of sand)
- A funnel
- Pebbles, shells, beads, or biodegradable glitter

GET CRAFTING:

1. Collect clear jars and bottles with lids.
2. Place a sheet of waxed paper on a cutting board. Spread sand over the paper.
3. Now roll a stick of chalk back and forth over the sand. Keep rolling until enough chalk has mixed with the sand to completely color the sand. Tip the sand into a small bowl.
4. Now repeat step 3 with other chalk colors.

5 Using a funnel, gently pour one color of sand into a jar. You can make the layer as thin or thick as you like. Then add a layer in a different color. Gently tap the jar between layers to help the sand settle. Keep adding layers.

6 You can fill the jar only with sand, or add other decorations, too. Try adding a layer of pretty pebbles. You can also place colorful beads, shells, or glitter in the jar.

7 When the jar is filled, press down on the sand firmly with your fingers. This will press the layers together as much as possible. Then place the lid on tightly.

MAKING ROCKS IN LAYERS

The process of making sedimentary rock is a little like nature making a sandwich from layers of sediment. However, the rocky sandwich can take thousands or millions of years to form!

It's easy to see the different layers in this sandstone sedimentary rock.

New sedimentary rock begins with a layer of sediment. Then, another layer of sediment settles on top. Then another and another. Very slowly, layer upon layer of sediment builds up.

All that rock weighs so much that the layers at the bottom are changed by the pressure. The sediments are so tightly pressed together that they actually join together to make solid rock.

This type of sedimentary rock is called limestone.

Making a Rock Sandwich

Layers of sediment can build up in many ways. For example, rainwater with tiny bits of rock in it might wash into a river. Then the river carries this sediment into a lake. Over millions of years, layers of sediment will build up at the bottom of the lake.

PEBBLE ARTWORK

Pebbles on a beach or in a garden can be arranged to make pictures and shapes. You can leave your pebble artwork in place for other people to spot and enjoy. You can also photograph it and turn it into a homemade greeting card.

You will need:

- Pebbles
- A bucket
- A flat surface, such as a beach or garden patio or terrace
- A digital camera
- Colorful construction paper or thin cardboard
- Scissors
- Glue
- Colored pens
- White printer paper
- A printer and computer, or a photo printer
- An adult to be your teammate and help with cutting, using the camera, and printing the photos

GET CRAFTING:

1. First, collect lots of pebbles in a bucket. Now it's time to get creative! Arrange the pebbles in your own patterns and designs on the flat surface.

2. When you have finished each picture, ask an adult to help you take a photograph of it.

3 Print out the photographs. You can print them big or small. Then ask an adult to help you cut them out.

4 Make greeting cards by folding pieces of construction paper or thin cardboard in half. Then stick pebble art photographs to the paper or cardboard.

5 You can write personal messages onto your cards, too!

HOW DOES METAMORPHIC ROCK FORM?

Metamorphic rock forms from other types of rock that have gone through huge changes called a metamorphosis.

Rocks can be pressed down under the weight of other rocks. They may also be baked by heat underground. Being heated and pressed together can change an igneous or sedimentary rock into something new—a metamorphic rock.

Sometimes, one type of metamorphic rock can change into a different type of metamorphic rock.

There are so many different types of rocks that people collect them. You can start a rock collection by looking in a backyard or at a beach.

These rocks are types of metamorphic rock.

gneiss

quartzite

marble

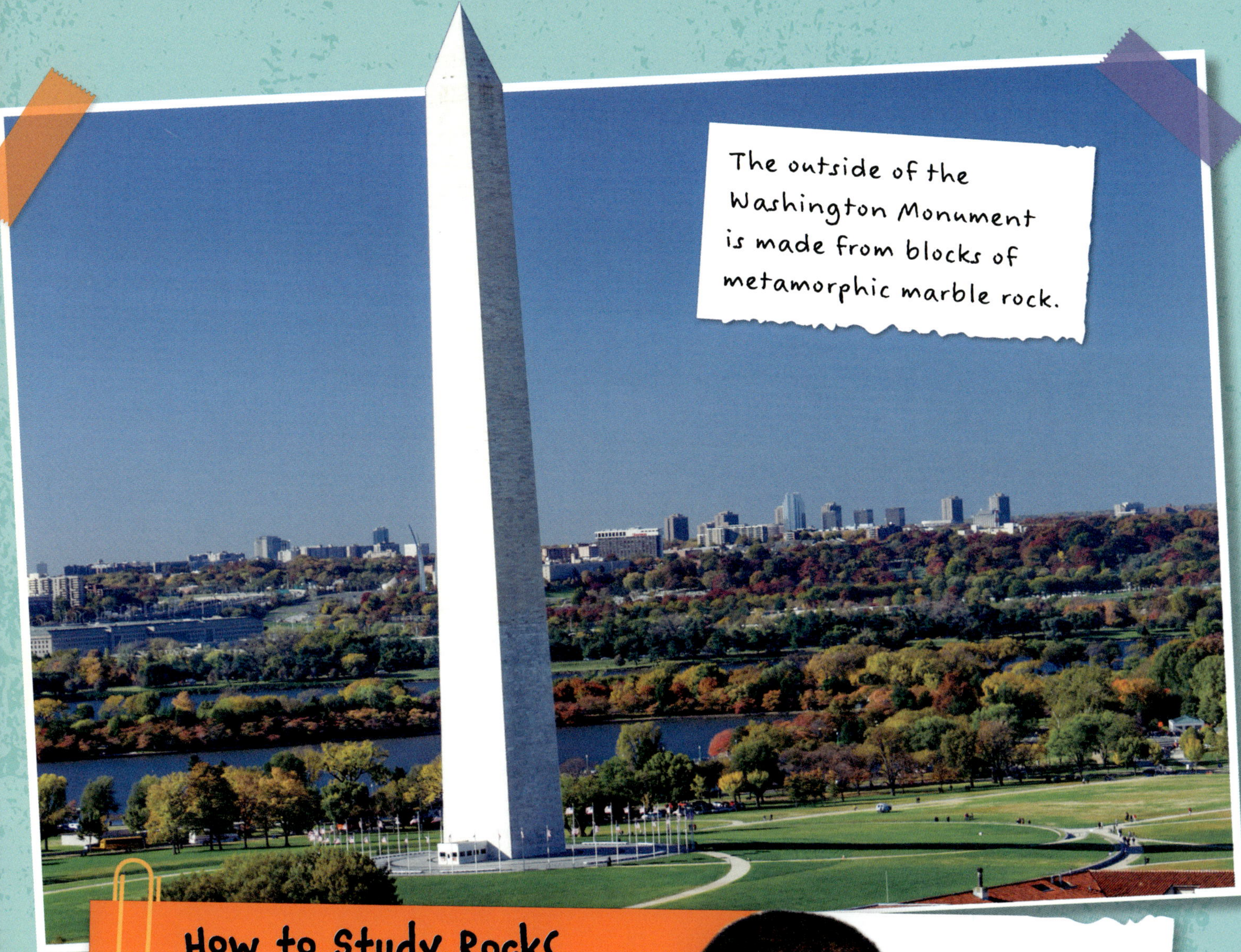

The outside of the Washington Monument is made from blocks of metamorphic marble rock.

How to Study Rocks

When you find a new rock, keep a record of where you found it. Then check out your rock.

- How much does it weigh?
- What is its size and shape?
- Is it colorful, dull, or shiny?
- Is it rough or smooth?
- How hard is it? Can you scratch it with your fingernail or a coin?

If you don't know what the rock is, borrow a rock identification book from the library.

ROCK-COLLECTING DISPLAY BOX

A rock collector needs a display box to show off their rocky finds. This is easy to make using just a cereal box and some egg cartons.

You will need:

- An empty cereal box
- Empty egg cartons
- Scissors
- Tape
- Paint
- Paintbrushes
- Glue
- An adult to help you with cutting

GET CRAFTING:

1. Cut one side from an empty cereal box. Then trim down the four sides of the box so that it forms a tray about 1 inch (2.5 cm) deep.

2. Stick the corners of the tray together with tape. Stick the tape inside the tray so it doesn't show.

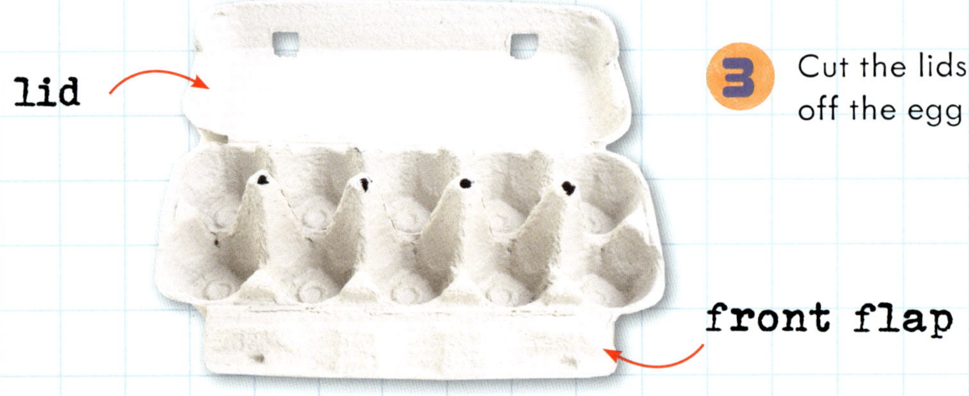

3. Cut the lids and front flaps off the egg cartons.

4 Now you need to fill the tray with egg cartons. You may need to cut some cartons in half or into smaller sections to completely fill the tray.

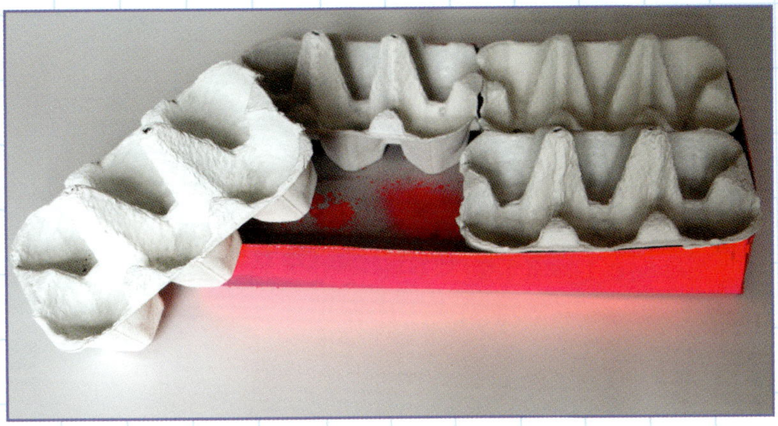

5 Take the egg cartons from the tray and paint them. White paint works well because it will show off the items in the display case.

6 Paint the cardboard tray in a bright color.

7 When all the paint has dried, cover the inside of the tray with glue. Put the egg cartons back into the tray and press them onto the glue.

8 Once the glue has dried, your display case is ready. Put the rocks you find into the case. You can also buy rocks for your collection from rock, craft, and hobby stores.

Rocks for sale in a rock shop

ALL ABOUT MINERALS

A rock is made of natural, solid substances called **minerals.** Some rocks are made of a mixture of several minerals. Others are formed from just one type of mineral.

The famous Half Dome rock in Yosemite National Park is made of an igneous rock called granite. The minerals that form granite are feldspar, quartz, mica, and hornblende.

Beautiful Shapes

Minerals sometimes grow in shapes called **crystals**. A crystal has straight edges and smooth sides, called faces. Salt is a type of mineral that forms in crystals. If you look at a grain of salt through a **microscope**, you can see its crystal shape.

Some minerals are so beautiful they are used to make jewelry. Diamonds, rubies, and emeralds are all minerals. Pieces of these minerals are removed from rocks. They are cut into shapes and polished. Then they are known as gemstones.

ruby crystals in rock

a cut and polished ruby gemstone

These minerals have been cut and polished to make gemstones.

diamond

opal

citrine

emerald

amethyst

sapphire

CREATE CRYSTALS

This next project shows you how to make holiday decorations by growing your own crystals. However, it's also a science experiment, so you must be extra careful with the materials you use.

You will need:

- Pipe cleaners
- Two pairs of rubber dishwashing gloves
- A clean, empty glass jar for each shape
- Borax crystals (available in the laundry aisle at the supermarket)
- A measuring cup
- Cold water
- A tablespoon
- Food coloring
- Pencils or chopsticks
- Boiling water
- An adult to boil and pour the water and handle the borax
- String

GET CRAFTING:

1. Bend the pipe cleaners into shapes of your choice.
2. Tie a piece of string to each shape.

3 Using cold water, measure how many cups of water each jar will hold.

4 Then ask an adult to fill each jar with boiling water. Next, add borax to each jar. For every cup of water, add 3 tablespoons of borax. So, if a jar holds two cups of water, add 6 tablespoons of borax.

5 Ask an adult to stir the boiling water and borax until all the borax has dissolved and the water looks clear.

6 If you want colored shapes, ask an adult to add two or three drops of food coloring to the water and stir.

WARNING

Borax crystals are poisonous and can cause serious illness if swallowed. They can also burn your skin. Be sure an adult performs the steps that involve pouring or mixing borax, and that both of you are wearing rubber gloves.

7 Tie each pipe cleaner shape to a pencil or chopstick.

8 Finally, ask an adult to dangle one shape into each jar. The pencil should rest over the opening of the jar, so the shape hangs in the water. The shape should not touch the bottom of the jar.

9 Leave the jars overnight. The next day, crystals will have formed on the pipe cleaner shapes! Have an adult help you remove the shapes from the water and allow them to dry. Be sure both of you are wearing gloves when you handle the wet crystals.

FINDING FOSSILS IN ROCKS

A rock may contain the fossils of a prehistoric animal or plant. But what needed to happen for a fossil to form?

When a prehistoric animal died, the soft parts of its body rotted away or were eaten by other animals. The remaining bones were then covered by floodwaters. The waters became a river that, over time, deposited layers of sediment on top of the bones.

Inside the sediment, water turned the bones into rocky minerals. Then, over tens of thousands of years, the layers of sediment were crushed and cemented together to make rock.

Deep inside the layers of rock, the animal's bones became rocky fossils.

Fossil Finds

Fossils have been found of dinosaurs, birds, fish, insects, plants, and even dinosaur droppings!

a turtle fossil

a fish fossil

fossilized plant leaves

a fossilized *Tyrannosaurus rex*

FANTASTIC FOSSILS

It took the fossils that scientists and fossil collectors sometimes discover in rocks millions of years to form. But by following these steps, you will be able to make your own rocky fossils in just 30 minutes!

You will need:

- Leaves, seashells, or any object that you want to fossilize
- Modeling clay
- Cooking oil
- A strip of cardboard about 1 inch (2.5 cm) wide
- A paper clip
- Plaster of Paris
- A bowl
- Water
- A spoon for mixing

GET CRAFTING:

1. Using your hands, roll out a lump of modeling clay so it is flat and smooth.

2. Press a seashell or leaf into the clay, then remove.

3. Rub a little cooking oil into the shape in the clay with your fingers.

4 Using the cardboard strip and paper clip, make a little collar, or wall, around the shape.

5 Put some plaster of Paris into the bowl, add some water, and start stirring. The mixture should be the thickness of pancake batter with no lumps. Keep adding plaster or water until the mix is right.

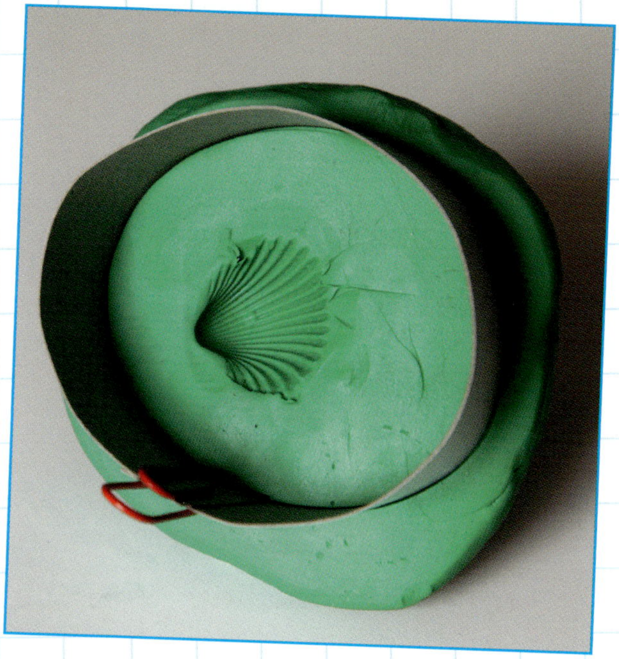

6 Spoon or pour the mix into the shape in the modeling clay and then fill the cardboard collar with plaster of Paris.

7 The plaster should set hard in about 30 minutes. Gently touch the plaster to find out if it is dry and hard. If it still feels soft, leave it for another 10 minutes and then try again.

8 When the plaster is hard and dry, gently remove the modeling clay from around the model. You will have a fossil of the object you pressed into the modeling clay!

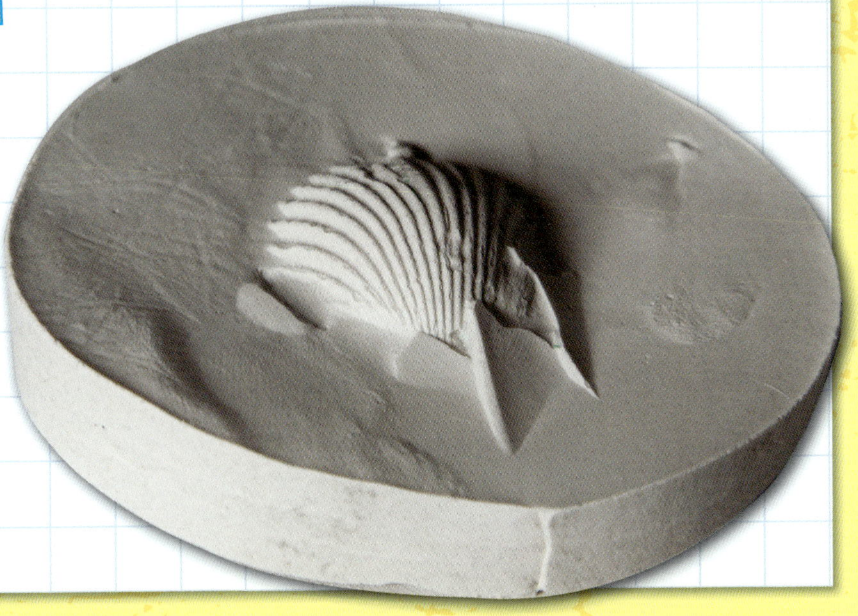

GLOSSARY

crust (KRUST)
The outer layer of Earth that is made of rock.

crystal (KRIS-tul)
A solid mineral that has formed in nature with a shape that has straight edges and smooth faces.

fossil (FAH-sul)
An imprint of an animal or plant's remains that has formed in rock over millions of years.

igneous rock (IG-nee-us ROK)
Rock made from magma or lava that has cooled and become hard.

lava (LAH-vuh)
Magma that has escaped from underground out of a volcano.

magma (MAG-muh)
Underground rock that has become so hot it melts.

metamorphic rock (meh-tuh-MOR-fik ROK)
Rock that has changed from one type to another because it has been pressed down upon by other rocks and heated underground.

microscope (MY-kruh-skohp)
A piece of equipment that allows a person to see a large view of an object that is too small to see with their eyes alone.

mineral (MIN-uh-rul)
A solid substance made in nature. Rocks are made from minerals.

sculpture (SKULP-cher)
A model made from a material such as rock or wood.

sediment (SEH-deh-ment)
Tiny pieces of rock that have been worn away from bigger rocks by forces such as waves or wind.

sedimentary rock (seh-deh-MEN-teh-ree ROK) Rock made from many layers of sediment that have been pressed so hard they join together and become solid.

volcano (vol-KAY-noh) A hole in Earth's crust through which magma, or lava, escapes. Over time, a mountain of rock made from cooled lava may build up around the hole.

Websites

https://www.amnh.org/dinosaurs

https://www.ducksters.com/science/rocks.php

https://kidsloverocks.com/educational-resources/

Publisher's note to parents and teachers: Our editors have reviewed the websites listed here to make sure they're suitable for students. However, websites may change frequently. Please note that students should always be supervised when they access the internet.

READ MORE

Anthony, William. *Create a Coastline (How to Build Our World)*. Minneapolis, MN: Bearport Publishing, 2022.

Morrison, Marie. *20 Things You Didn't Know About Rocks and Gems (Did You Know? Earth Science)*. New York, NY: Rosen Publishing, 2023.

Owen, Ruth. *Rocks: Let's Investigate (Science Essentials)*. Minneapolis, MN: Ruby Tuesday Books, 2021

INDEX